WHAT ARE LEAF-FROGS?

THE PHYLLOMEDUSINES

The interest in keeping reptiles and amphibians as pets has increased markedly over the last decade, resulting in a fascination with some truly unusual and often quite rare species. One of the oddest and certainly most colorful is the species usually called the Red-eyed Treefrog, *Agalychnis callidryas*, from Central America. This frog appears in all types of hobby literature, on tee-shirts, mugs, window hangings, pins, and even wallpaper, and it is hard to name a natural history magazine that doesn't run a picture of it on the cover at least every other year. It is the most commonly seen leaf-frog or phyllomedusine.

The treefrogs, family Hylidae, long have been familiar herp pets, but of the over 500 American species (in at least 50 genera) only a few have ever been really common, and even fewer have been bred in captivity with any regularity. The hylids are a very diverse family, and often several subfamilies are recognized. One of these subfamilies, the Phyllomedusinae, has some especially odd and often extremely colorful members. Often called monkey frogs, walking treefrogs, or leaf-frogs, the subfamily contains several types of small to rather large frogs that all share a cat-like, vertically elliptical pupil in an often brilliantly colored eye (most other treefrogs have a horizontally elliptical pupil).

In the rest of their structure the phyllomedusines are quite variable, ranging from tiny, delicate frogs with slender, almost muscle-less legs and fingers without climbing discs to heavy-bodied species with gigantic climbing discs connected by thick webs. Often there are parotoid glands under the skin behind the eyes and along the side of the back much as in toads, while some species are thin-skinned and lack any swollen glands on the back. Species with webbed feet and large

PHOTO BY W. P. MARA.

The Red-eyed Leaf-frog, *Agalychnis callidryas*, (often called the Red-eyed Treefrog) undoubtedly is one of the most popular frog pets in the world. Its toy-like appearance makes it an appealing subject for all sorts of "herp-art" pieces, including tee-shirts, mugs, and attractive little sculptures like the one shown here.

PHOTO BY D. DUBE, COURTESY NEW ENGLAND REPTILES.

Most of the leaf frogs are bright green during the day, some turning brown at night. Many have intricate patterns along the sides made up of colorful bars and/or spots. The red eye that is so well-known in the Red-eyed Leaf-frog, *Agalychnis callidryas*, is not consistent in the leaf-frog group (a subfamily known as the Phyllomedusinae).

climbing discs can leap much like a normal treefrog, while species with no webbing and no discs often walk with the body held high off the ground or climb hand-over-hand like a lemur or other primitive primate (thus the names walking treefrogs and monkey frogs). Virtually all the species are bright green in life during the day, often becoming brown at night, and most have brilliant flash-colors in the hidden parts of the thigh. Many have complicated patterns of bars and spots on the sides, and often the fingers and toes are brightly colored.

Technically these frogs share an unusual chromosome number (2N = 26) and a very odd pigment known as rhodomelanin that otherwise is found only in some Australian treefrogs of the genus *Litoria*. All lay their eggs in tight clusters on a leaf or inside the overlapping leaf bases of tropical plants and not directly in the water. (Recently there have been hints that a few species may lay their eggs at the water's edge, but this would be highly exceptional.) Though their tadpoles often are modified, they all have the spiracle (exit pore for water from the gills) located to the left of the midline of the belly rather than on the lower side as in most other treefrogs.

THE GENERA

The 48 currently-recognized species of phyllomedusines are, as already mentioned, very varied in structure, but they have proved difficult to break into distinct genera. As a general rule, there is no problem recognizing the Central American leaf-frogs of the genus *Agalychnis*, which have webbed feet, large climbing discs, non-opposable fingers, a shallow skull, and bright green backs combined with bright yellow or red eyes. These are the leaf-frogs most often seen in captivity because they occur in areas that are easy to collect from, often are very abundant at breeding congresses, are large and robust, and survive at least moderate periods in tall, heavily planted terraria.

There currently are 28 species in the genus *Phyllomedusa* (shown is *P. hypocondrialis*), most being found in South America (two occur in Central America). Some examples of the genus occasionally turn up in the herpetocultural trade, but most are virtually unknown to hobbyists.

Along the western coast of Mexico, often in very dry habitats, is found the only species of *Pachymedusa*, a large green frog with a white belly, rather small climbing discs, shallow webbing between the fingers and toes, and a deep skull. Occasionally captive-bred, it is well-studied in nature but has a checkered history in the terrarium hobby.

South America is the home of some 39 species of large to small, green to yellow or brown, plain to spotted, translucent to gaudy frogs placed in *Phyllomedusa* and three satellite genera. The three satellite genera, *Hylomantis, Phasmahyla,* and *Phrynomedusa,* are known only from Brazil, which does not allow legal exportation of its frogs for the terrarium hobby. They are unavailable to the average hobbyist, or even most advanced hobbyists, and any in the hobby are of doubtful legality. Twenty-eight species of varied frogs are placed in *Phyllomedusa*, which ranges from Central America (only two species, one very rare) to Argentina. All the species have little or no webbing between the fingers and toes and often have rather small or no climbing discs. In some species the first and second fingers and toes are shifted a bit in position so they are opposable like a human thumb and first finger, allowing the frogs to climb (very slowly) over-hand; these species lack climbing discs, as you might expect. At the extremes of the genus are tiny, plainly colored (green and bluish or pinkish) frogs with virtually no muscle mass on the legs and others over 4 inches long with gigantic parotoid glands under the skin behind the eyes, relatively large climbing discs, and heavily muscled legs.

A CHECKLIST

The following listing of species is presented for convenience of reference. Much work has been done lately on the leaf-frogs of South America, and their generic classification is in a state of flux. Additionally, several undescribed species are known to exist and several names now considered synonyms probably will be resurrected as valid species in the near future. As usual with any checklist, expect the names to change a bit.

Subfamily PHYLLOMEDUSINAE
Leaf-frogs
AGALYCHNIS Cope, 1864 [type: *callidryas*]
  A. annae (Duellman, 1963)
  Blue-sided Leaf-frog. Costa Rica.
  A. calcarifer Boulenger, 1902
  Splendid Leaf-frog. Costa Rica to Ecuador.
  A. callidryas (Cope, 1862)
  Red-eyed Leaf-frog. Mexico to Panama.
  A. craspedopus (Funkhouser, 1957)
  Fringed Leaf-frog. Amazonian Ecuador and Peru.

Facing Page: The Blue-sided Leaf-frog, *Agalychnis annae*, is one of the larger phyllomedusines, the males growing to around 3 inches and the females to about 3.5. Photo by R. D. Bartlett.

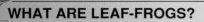

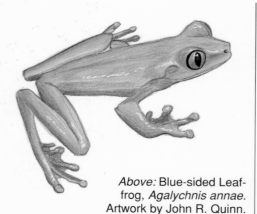

Above: Blue-sided Leaf-frog, *Agalychnis annae.* Artwork by John R. Quinn.

A. litodryas (Duellman & Trueb, 1967)

Pink-sided Leaf-frog. Panama to Ecuador.

A. moreleti (Dumeril, 1853)

Orange-sided Leaf-frog. Mexico to Guatemala and El Salvador.

A. saltator Taylor, 1955

Misfit Leaf-frog. Nicaragua and Costa Rica.

A. spurrelli Boulenger, 1913

Gliding Leaf-frog. Costa Rica to Colombia.

HYLOMANTIS Peters, 1872 [type: *aspera*]

Hylomantis aspera Peters, 1872

Rough Leaf-frog. Brazil.

Hylomantis granulosa (Cruz, 1988)

Granular Leaf-frog. Brazil.

PACHYMEDUSA Duellman, 1968 [type: *dacnicolor*]

Pachymedusa dacnicolor (Cope, 1864)

Mexican Leaf-frog. Mexico.

PHASMAHYLA Cruz, 1990 [type: *guttata*]

PHOTO BY K. H. SWITAK

The Red-eyed Leaf-frog, *Agalychnis callidryas*, has an extensive geographical range, from southeastern Mexico to Panama south to the Colombian border. Interestingly, throughout this range the animal shows a great deal of color and pattern variation.

Below: Splendid Leaf-frog, *Agalychnis calcarifer.* Artwork by John R. Quinn.

Above: Misfit Leaf-frog, *Agalychnis saltator.* Artwork by John R. Quinn.

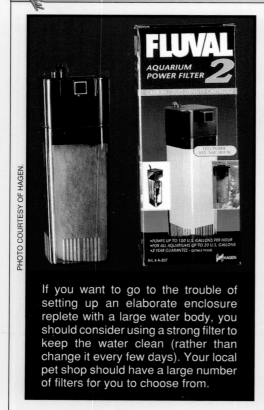

If you want to go to the trouble of setting up an elaborate enclosure replete with a large water body, you should consider using a strong filter to keep the water clean (rather than change it every few days). Your local pet shop should have a large number of filters for you to choose from.

upper wall of the terrarium and one for measuring the water temperature). This will save you from making repeated trips to the pet shop as the requirements of the frogs change from the dry, cool resting period to the wet, warmer breeding period.

The terrarium can be quite complicated. Basically, the bottom should be covered with a deep layer (3 to 4 inches) of moisture-holding substrate such as bark mulch, orchid bark, or a peat moss mix. To prevent stagnation, it is best to put a layer of charcoal under the substrate or use a piece of open-mesh egg crate (covering for fluorescent lamps) on the bottom. If you can, it is best to have in the tank an area of open water that is filtered with a sponge

filter (if small) or an undergravel filter (if larger). The water should be dechlorinated to prevent possible skin irritation.

Successfully keeping Red-eyes means that you will have to mist the terrarium on a regular basis. Mist the terrarium heavily each morning and each evening before the lights go out. However, there should be as little condensation as possible at the top of the terrarium, thus the need for a screened lid. By covering the screen with plastic or foil, you can control the ventilation and the condensation; the less screening left open, the more humid the terrarium will remain and the less fresh air will circulate. Leaf-frogs need fresh air most of the year, and some will not take high humidities if not breeding. During breeding season, of course, you may have to take measures to

There are many different types of filters designed to suit all types of setups. Do yourself a favor and work up a pretty good idea of which one you'll need before making your purchase.

Organic substrates like crushed bark are ideal for naturalistic setups. Most are easy to work with, pleasing to the eye, and can be bought in bulk quantities.

Although red-eyes do not need much light (and actively avoid the light most of the time), the plants will need correct fluorescent lighting to thrive.

LIGHTS AND HEATERS

Lighting for the terrarium should be set up to satisfy primarily the plants and only secondarily the frogs. Though some keepers feel that tadpoles and adult frogs need at least some ultraviolet light, there is no doubt that the frogs shun the light during the day and are less stressed if kept dark. Just providing lighting for the plants should be sufficient.

Many keepers use a red or blue incandescent light of about 15 to

A large water body can be warmed quite efficiently with the help of a fully submersible heater. Such heaters are offered in a variety of sizes and wattages and usually are quite affordable.

ensure higher humidities, but we'll talk about that later.

PLANTS

Red-eyes are arboreal frogs that seldom rest on the ground, so they must be provided with plants in which to hide. Use large-leafed, hardy plants that can support the weight of the frogs as they move around at night. Anthuriums, philodendrons, and smooth bromeliads are suitable and also provide color and variety in the terrarium. The plants should be left in their pots and just buried in the bedding. This way they can be taken out of the terrarium every month or so and rested on a windowsill while substitutes take their place in the terrarium.

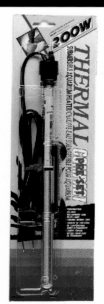

no problem going in and out to feed. The largest crickets fed should not be wider than the mouth of the frog.

All crickets should be both gut-loaded (fed on foods high in vitamins and minerals) and, at least once a week, also covered with powdered vitamins by shaking in a plastic bag. (For details of

Many leaf-frogs seem to like moths. These can be cultured simply by purchasing waxworms and allowing them to mature.

food of many leaf-frogs. These can be collected from the wild by putting a white sheet under a bright light on summer nights or by allowing waxworms to mature into the adult moths.

Harder foods such as mealworms are not suggested for leaf-frogs. However, small beetles are acceptable and can be either collected or raised. Cultures of flour beetles sometimes are available and should provide both

Most leaf-frogs eat crickets, and crickets are made more nutritious when maintained on a high-calcium diet. This practice is known as "gut-loading" and should be utilized by all keepers.

Flies can be collected in the wild and will be eagerly accepted by most leaf-frogs. Be careful, though, of *where* you collect your flies; areas that have been treated with pesticides should be avoided.

feeding and breeding crickets, see *Feeding Insect-feeding Lizards* by David Zoffer, T.F.H.)

Moths seem to be a preferred

PHOTO BY W. P. MARA

Crickets undoubtedly are the most commonly offered leaf-frog food. They can be purchased in bulk at most pet shops and are reasonably priced.

suitable larvae and adults for your frogs. Cultured houseflies (raised in bran or oatmeal, not rotten meat) also are an excellent food; adults are quite edible but larvae are too tough-skinned for most frogs. Giant fruitflies can also be cultured but are hard to feed because they escape easily from the terrarium.

ACTIVITY PATTERNS

Agalychnis callidryas and other leaf-frogs are very much creatures of the night. They spend the day sleeping under cover, usually under leaves of shrubs or trees. Most *Agalychnis* live high in the forest canopy, but many *Phyllomedusa* live in shrubs only a few feet above the ground, and one species (*Phyllomedusa atelopoides*, the Toady Leaf-frog) is terrestrial except when breeding. They rest with their legs pulled tightly against the body to prevent water loss. If disturbed during the day they usually react slowly to predators, either leaping toward the ground (*Agalychnis*) or climbing or walking away. In either case, the frogs display the bright colors hidden in the legs, the flash-colors, to distract the predator for a few seconds during the escape.

Activity usually begins when the sun goes down and continues over much of the night. The frogs actively search through the leaves for suitable insect prey. Mating also occurs at night.

This simple activity period means that you should feed the frogs when the lights go out, otherwise it will go to waste. Additionally, light cycles with much over 12 hours of daylight might be stressful to the frog because they don't allow enough time for feeding and other activities. If you want to see your leaf-frog actively moving around, you probably will have to use the recommended red or blue light. The terrarium, of course, should not be kept in a sunny area.

BREEDING LEAF-FROGS

PREPARING THE FROGS

To successfully breed the Red-eyed Leaf-frog, you have to prepare both the frogs and the terrarium. This is a species that breeds during the Central American rainy season and then becomes less active or disappears for the rest of the year when it becomes relatively drier. You should try to mimic this cycle in the terrarium.

Starting in November or December, gradually let the humidity in the terrarium drop to about 50% (assuming you have kept it at 90% or so as many keepers recommend) over a period of two or three weeks. At the same time let the temperature drop by about 10° from normal (i.e., 70 to 75°F, 21 to 24°C, during the day, down to 60°F, 16°C, at night). If you wish, you also can reduce the hours of daylight, but this is not essential; just make sure the terrarium is kept out of the light yet the plants still have enough light to live. The frogs will continue to feed under these conditions though at a slower pace. They should not become completely inactive.

Maintain the frogs under these dry conditions for about three months, then begin to mist the terrarium heavily each day and raise the temperature. By spring the frogs should be fully active and eating heavily. Females are generally a bit larger than males and should be swelling with eggs. Males call at sunset when they become active. The call is a slow "chock" in this species, but in many other leaf-frogs it is much higher and faster, more like cricket chirps. Sexually active male leaf-frogs have brown nuptial pads on the palm and fingers that are absent in females.

If at all possible, you should try to maintain a colony of Red-eyes for breeding purposes. There is much observational evidence that the frogs breed more freely if several males are present to call and attract females. At least four frogs should be present in the breeding terrarium, all having gone through the drying period. The more frogs you have, the more chances for successfully getting strong, healthy tadpoles.

PREPARING THE TERRARIUM

Actually, terrarium might be the wrong word for the breeding enclosure for Red-eyed Leaf-frogs. A tank set up for breeding large numbers of Red-eyes is almost as much water surface as it is land. Misting seems to be the secret, and misting means a lot of water in the bottom of the terrarium. Thus, after bringing the frogs out of dryness into active feeding and calling, you should either move

Facing Page: Red-eyed Leaf-frogs are not easy to breed in captivity, but they're not impossible either. In the wild, they breed only during what is known as the rainy season, and a keeper needs to replicate the subtle climatic changes of this season if he or she wants results. Photo by H. Zimmermann.

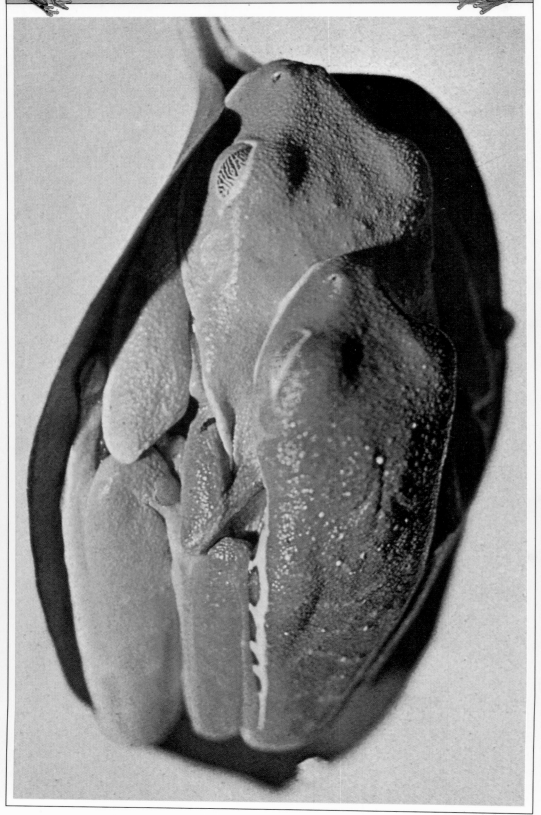

PHOTO BY R. S. SIMMONS.

Although a remarkably attractive leaf-frog with a very large range, the Splendid Leaf-frog, *Agalychnis calcarifer*, rarely finds its way into the herpetocultural hobby. It gets its species name from the pointed flap of skin on its heel, known as a calcar.

with *A. moreleti* in the past but differs strikingly in color. As usual, it breeds in woodland pools and lays its egg masses on overhanging leaves. The masses usually number about 50 to 150 eggs. Blue-sided Leaf-frogs are imported on an irregular basis and occasionally have been bred in captivity, but they never are common and have a reputation as a delicate species subject to various fungal and bacterial infections. Be careful when purchasing specimens that they are not wounded or abraded in any way.

SPLENDID LEAF-FROG
Agalychnis calcarifer

This stunning leaf-frog is rarely collected though it has a large range in the humid lowlands of Central America (Caribbean Costa Rica and Panama) into northwestern South America (Pacific Colombia and Ecuador). The presence of a short, pointed skin flap (the calcar) on the heel is shared only with the even rarer Fringed Leaf-frog, which has extensive fringing on all the limbs. The sides, belly, and hidden surfaces of the limbs are bright yellow or orange with narrow irregular black vertical bars, while the back is dark green, often with whitish flecks. The eye appears to be mostly pale yellow. A moderate-sized species (males 2.5 inches, females 3 inches), it remains poorly known and seldom is seen in captivity; it would seem to be one of the hidden inhabitants of the forest canopy. It has been found breeding in pools in fallen logs, the small egg clutch (16 eggs reported in one instance) adhering to an overhanging dead leaf.

RED-EYED LEAF-FROG
Agalychnis callidryas

The Red-eye is the only common leaf-frog in captivity, and it is both collected heavily from the wild and captive-bred. It has an extensive range from southeastern Mexico to Panama right to the Colombian border and shows great variation in details of color pattern over its range. Specimens from Caribbean Nicaragua and Costa Rica have blue thighs and a distinct white to pale yellow stripe on the side connecting the tops of the yellow to white vertical bars, while specimens from Mexico and Honduras have orange thighs and no white stripe on the side above the white bars. A third pattern in some specimens from Panama has both blue and orange on the thighs and T-shaped bars on the sides. As a rule, there are more

Undoubtedly the most popular of the phyllomedusines, the Red-eyed Leaf-frog, *Agalychnis callidryas*, probably is *not* the easiest one to maintain in captivity. It is susceptible to all sorts of health problems, and many specimens refuse to eat. When purchasing one, be sure it already is as close to "perfect" as possible.

PHOTO BY MELLA PANZELLA.

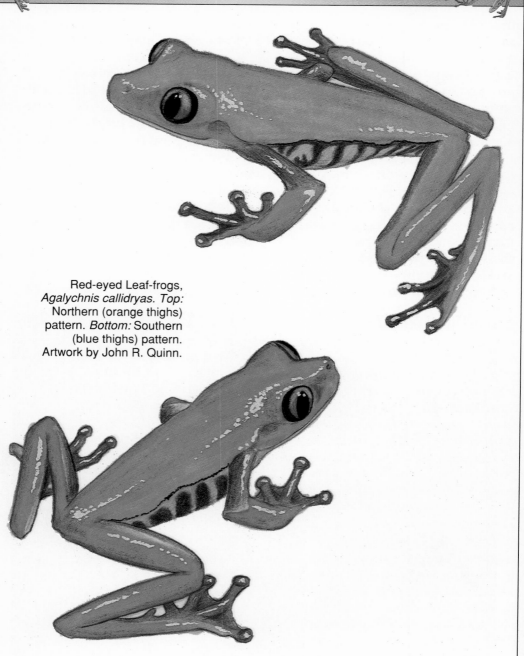

Red-eyed Leaf-frogs,
Agalychnis callidryas. Top:
Northern (orange thighs)
pattern. *Bottom:* Southern
(blue thighs) pattern.
Artwork by John R. Quinn.

pale vertical bars on the side in
specimens from Panama than
from Mexico. Many specimens
have irregular white flecks or
spots on the back, and some from
Costa Rica have traces of dark
green bars on the back as well.
Several synonyms are available

for this species in case it ever is decided that subspecies are recognizable based on patterns, including *helenae* for specimens from Nicaragua and Costa Rica and *taylori* for those from Mexico. (Please note that these names should not be used until a competent herpetologist has studied variation in this species.) The type locality is Darien, Panama, by the way. Males are about 2 inches long, with females larger, as usual in frogs, at nearly 3 inches. Specimens from the northern part of the range average smaller than those from the south. The combination of brilliant red eye and vertical white to pale yellow striping on the side is unique.

This species commonly is collected from the central and southern parts of the range, so most specimens seen in pet shops have bright blue legs and arms. Always select specimens that are as perfect as possible, because infections spreading from small abrasions are not uncommon. Captive-bred specimens are uncommon but available if you look hard enough. In nature the species breeds in pools during the rainy season, laying its eggs on overhanging leaves and vines. During the day and during the dry season it lives in the forest canopy, often hiding in palm fronds. The greenish yolk turns yellowish as development progresses. It takes several days to a few weeks for froglets to develop the bright colors (including the eye) of the adult.

Here's a familiar sight to anyone who's ever kept a Red-eyed Leaf-frog. When they're not nestled behind a heavy leaf or crawling along the ground in search of prey, Red-eyes will stick themselves to the walls of their enclosure. As you might be able to guess, they are excellent climbers.

FRINGED LEAF-FROG
Agalychnis craspedopus

The most bizarre leaf-frog and one of the most beautiful, the Fringed Leaf-frog remains rare and poorly known. Colored much like the Splendid Leaf-frog (orange on the sides and belly, with blackish vertical bars on the sides), this species can be instantly recognized by the presence of not only a calcar on the heel but broad scalloped fleshy fringes on the legs, unique in the subfamily. The back is deep green with a very variable pattern of grayish white blotches and streaks that mimic a lichen background; presumably the frog blends well with tree trunks and

BRAZILIAN ODDBALLS

Brazil has many leaf-frogs that seem not to be found elsewhere, but this short chapter is devoted to the seldom-seen species of *Hylomantis, Phasmahyla*, and *Phrynomedusa*. Because all the species of these recently recognized genera are known only from Brazil, which currently does not allow legal exportation of its frogs, they are virtually unknown to hobbyists. Even the scientific works leave a lot to be desired, and it is safe to say that most of the species are among the least known of tropical frogs.

I can't say much about the two species of *Hylomantis* because they are so obscure they remain largely unknown. Both species are from northeastern Brazil in the state of Pernambuco. They have relatively rough skin for leaf-frogs and the tadpoles are not strongly modified for a stream existence. I doubt that they ever are present in the terrarium hobby.

Above: Bicolored Leaf-frog, *Phrynomedusa marginata*. Artwork by John R. Quinn.

PHRYNOMEDUSA

Phrynomedusa is an interesting group of rather odd leaf-frogs restricted to southeastern Brazil. The genus is recognized by the long, pointed flaps of skin (calcars) on the heels of the hind legs in combination with partially webbed hind feet. The eggs sometimes are deposited in crevices in trees and small pools of water in fallen logs. In addition, the tadpoles have papillae at the anterior edge of the mouth disc, an unusual feature in leaf-frogs. Only the Bicolored Leaf-frog, *Phrynomedusa marginata*, is known in the hobby, and it certainly is one of the rarer species.

This is a pretty little species about 1.5 inches long. It is sharply bicolored, bright green above (brown at night) defined by a thin white line that runs from the snout to the thigh, and pale brown on the side, from the snout to the thigh. The belly is whitish, the limbs are green above and brownish orange on the hidden surfaces, and the bright golden eye has a distinct dusky brownish band running through it. The hind feet are partially webbed. The Bicolored Leaf-frog is an inhabitant of bromeliads and low shrubs along rapid mountain streams like most of the southeastern Brazilian oddballs. It tolerates temperatures as low as 59°F (15°C), making it a potentially valuable terrarium species if it should become available. The large eggs are laid in small clusters (30 to 45 eggs) in crevices in palms above the stream edges. The tadpoles hatch in about two weeks and mature in about two months. Fully developed tadpoles have a tail that is darkly mottled, with a long, fine tip. The froglet has a dark brown band along the side much like the adult.

If kept at normal terrarium temperatures this frog is subject to various bacterial and fungal infections, which also is true of other cool mountain Brazilian frogs. This must be kept in mind if you should ever run across the frog or one of its relatives in the trade.

PHASMAHYLA

Also found only in the mountains of southeastern Brazil are the species of *Phasmahyla*, rather delicate-looking species with short snouts and large, bulging greenish eyes. The feet are virtually without webs and the first and second toes are similar in size and set off a bit from the others. There are small calcars on the heels and the skin of the back often appears rough or finely warty. The tadpoles are quite distinctive, the edges of the mouth disc being greatly enlarged into two up-turned lobes forming a funnel that helps the larva feed from the surface of the water. Both adults and tadpoles are

Above:
Spotted Leaf-frog, *Phasmahyla guttata.* Artwork by John R. Quinn.

nocturnal, hiding during the day in bromeliads along streams (adults) or under rocks in the streams (tadpoles).

The Mottled Leaf-frog, *Phasmahyla exilis*, has been bred in captivity. Like the other species of the genus, males are significantly smaller than females, about 1.5 inches versus almost 2 inches. In *P. exilis* the back is flecked or mottled with small to large grayish or brownish spots on a green background and the sides are heavily spotted with brown on yellow. This species lays its 20 to 40 large eggs on a leaf hanging over the water and

Below: Mottled Leaf-frog, *Phasmahyla exilis.* Artwork by John R. Quinn.

then turns over the edges of the leaf to enclose the eggs in a loose tube. The eggs hatch in about two weeks. The tadpoles develop slowly because of the low water temperatures in their native streams.

Very similar to the Mottled Leaf-frog are the Spotted Leaf-frog, *P. guttata*, from mountains outside Rio de Janeiro and the Chocolate-footed Leaf-frog, *P. cochranae*, from outside Sao Paulo. The two species are very similar in structure to each other as well as to the Mottled Leaf-frog but differ in color. In *P. guttata* the plain green back (brown at night) is sharply set off from the yellow sides and belly, though there are a few brownish spots along the sides and on the hidden surfaces of the legs. *P. cochranae* is more brightly colored, with many bright chocolate brown spots, often fused into broken lines or blotches, on the hands and feet and the hidden surfaces of the legs. Both species live near cool mountain streams, their funnel-mouthed tadpoles living in deeper pools and coming out at night.

It's a pity that more Brazilian oddballs have not reached the terrarium hobby. Brazilian laws do allow some animals to leave the country for legitimate scientific purposes such as laboratory and zoo research and breeding experiments. Such legitimate research often has been the route by which very unusual animals eventually have entered the household terrarium, so there is some hope for these frogs. At the moment, however, they remain unknowns unavailable to hobbyists and true enigmas.

Above: Toady Leaf-frog, *Phyllomedusa atelopoides.* Artwork by John R. Quinn.

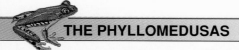

THE PHYLLOMEDUSAS

Phyllomedusa is a genus that cannot really be defined by modern methods; it simply is what is left over after the other genera are removed, thus it is what is known as a composite or paraphyletic group. Certainly it contains several groups of species that vary greatly in size, foot structure, and color patterns, each of which might eventually be separated as a full genus. For the moment, however, it is defined by having feet that are not webbed and tadpoles that are not highly specialized. The eye is silvery white to yellow, golden tan, or even greenish, but not bright red. The range of the genus extends from Costa Rica and Panama (only two species are recognized from Central America) south through most of South America to Argentina, a range encompassing every type of habitat from rainforest to dry prairies. As a general rule, the frogs lay masses of eggs in leaves suspended over temporary or permanent pools, the resulting tadpoles feeding from the surface while "standing" nearly vertically below the surface. Most males produce weak cricket-like chirps or low "chocks" and thus are not conspicuous or easy to collect except when breeding.

TOADY LEAF-FROG
Phyllomedusa atelopoides

A unique leaf-frog that lives on the ground and only climbs into low vegetation when breeding, the Toady Leaf-frog is small (males 1.5 inches, females a bit under 2 inches) and has a rather toad-like body with short legs with stubby digits without climbing discs. The coloration is very simple, basically purplish brown with small, irregular green flecks on the back and bluish white on the side and belly. There may be a fine dark purplish network on the belly. The eye is silvery gray with little black specks. Females lay clutches of about 20 whitish eggs that are encased in a folded leaf. There are many water-filled yolkless eggs mixed with the fertile eggs. Hatching takes about two weeks. Known only from the Iquitos region of Peru, where it seldom is collected, it is active at night and seldom is found more than a foot or two above the ground.

RETICULATED LEAF-FROG
Phyllomedusa ayeaye

The Reticulated Leaf-frog is a beautiful and distinctively patterned species closely related to *Phyllomedusa hypocondrialis* and *P. rohdei*. Described from the state of Minas Gerais, southeastern Brazil, it is a small species (about 1.5 inches long) that is green on the back and the exposed parts of the limbs, becoming brilliant scarlet to orange on the side and all hidden surfaces of the arms and legs. What makes it unique is the black reticulation that covers the entire side and hidden parts of the legs, extending onto the belly. The reticulations isolate spots of orange in the groin (much as in *P. rohdei*) and begin to break up and become weaker on the edges of the belly. The belly is salmon to pinkish, darkest in the center, becoming whitish on the throat. Little is known of its natural history, but it certainly would make a fascinating addition to the hobby if it ever were to become available.

PURPLE-SIDED LEAF-FROG
Phyllomedusa baltea

Seemingly restricted to the Serrania de Sira range in central Peru, the Purple-sided Leaf-frog is bright green above and purple on the belly, side, and hidden surfaces of the limbs. There are a narrow salmon stripe from the eye back toward the groin and fine white spots on the belly. The simple and bright color scheme is distinctive, though the species seems to be related to *Phyllomedusa perinesos*. Males are about 1.5 inches long, females 2 inches. Little is known of the natural history of this species other than the type specimens were taken from vegetation around a pond in the rainforest. The Purple-sided Leaf-frog occurs over 600 miles south of the range of its closest relatives.

Although popular in the herpetocultural hobby, the Giant Monkey Frog, *Phyllomedusa bicolor*, usually does not do well in captivity. This perhaps is a shame for aspiring breeders since the females can lay up to 2000 eggs at a time!

PHOTO BY PAUL FREED.

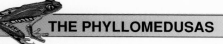

GIANT MONKEY FROG
Phyllomedusa bicolor

The true giant of leaf-frogs, *Phyllomedusa bicolor* was the first species of the subfamily to be described and it still is one of the best-known of the entire group. Unfortunately it is delicate in captivity and does not thrive when it is imported. It is found over much of northern and central South America from Colombia to the Guianas and Peru to Brazil, but apparently not in Ecuador. Adults are all around 4 inches in length (males 3.75 to 4.5 inches, females to almost 5 inches) and are stout and heavily built, with large hands and feet and large climbing discs. There is a large, toad-like parotoid gland behind the eye, while the skin of the back is rough and contains small, hard plates. The back, sides of the head, and tops of the limbs are bright green, while the throat and chest as well as outer parts of the limbs are grayish; the belly is dull orange. Along the side is a narrow reddish brown band that extends onto the hidden surfaces of the hind legs and contains many small but distinct rounded white spots outlined with black. The lower lip has a few white spots as well, and so does the base of the arm. The eye is silvery gray. No other frog can be confused with this species.

A big frog has the opportunity to lay many eggs, and the Giant Monkey Frog lives up to its potential. Females lay up to 2000 eggs at a time on the (obviously large) leaf of a plant overhanging the water. The edges of the leaf are rolled over to protect the nest and produce a rather conical egg cluster. There are many small water-filled yolkless eggs at the top and bottom of the nest. Hatching occurs in about eight to ten days. The time to metamorphosis is six to eight weeks at a temperature of 80°F (26°C) or better, the froglets being about an inch in length. Young raised in captivity fed on small crickets. Curiously, at first the young exhibited a color change from day (green) to night (brown) as in many smaller species of the genus. Red-leg disease (an *Aeromonas hydrophila* infection) proved to be a problem, and overall survivorship in captivity was low. This serves to reaffirm the fact that most leaf-frogs, no matter how common and widely distributed in nature, are delicate terrarium inmates.

The skin secretions of the Giant Monkey Frog contain a real cocktail of various drugs that sometimes have strong effects on humans. Some South American tribes use secretions from the frog during rites of passage to adulthood, as "medicine" to ensure a successful hunt, and also as a stimulant. Commonly the frog is tortured a bit (though not fatally) to produce the secretions, which are removed and mixed with saliva. The mixture is worked into the skin with a sharp twig, producing a permanent welt or scar. After undergoing a period of painful abdominal cramps, the user arises strengthened, clear-headed, and happy, ready to work harder or just enjoy the day more. This is one of the many frogs that possess great pharmaceutical interest, at least until the various chemicals in the skin are synthesized in the laboratory.

RED-RIMMED LEAF-FROG
Phyllomedusa boliviana

This large frog often has been called *Phyllomedusa pailona* in Argentine literature, but it seems that *P. boliviana* is the proper name. Known only from southern Bolivia and northern Argentina plus adjacent Brazil, it lives in low shrubs near permanent and temporary ponds in prairie-like habitats. Males are about 1.5 inches long, females 3 inches. The body is robust, there is a long parotoid gland behind the eye, and the snout slopes downward from the nostrils. The eye is almost black, but the upper eyelid is distinctly edged with red. As usual, the back and upper parts of the limbs are bright green; the belly is gray, with many yellow blotches; and the hidden surfaces of the legs are pale yellowish green with an orange tint. There is a more-or-less distinct pale stripe on the sides that often has red or brownish tubercles and spots within it. The species lays clutches of about 100 to 150 eggs on a leaf above the water and folds the edges of the leaf over the eggs. There are a few water-filled yolkless eggs at each end of the egg mass. I've seen no information on development of the eggs or keeping this species in captivity.

WARTY LEAF-FROG
Phyllomedusa buckleyi

This poorly known leaf-frog from Amazonian Ecuador usually has a distinct calcar on the heels and rough, warty skin. Adults are about 2 inches long (females longer than males), green above (brown at night) with purplish flecks, pale orange below and on the hidden surfaces of the limbs. The eye is creamy silver. Virtually nothing has been reported on the natural history of this species, though recently it was discovered that the eggs are laid on sedges at the surface of the water in temporary ponds, so far a unique behavior in the group. The species long was called *Phyllomedusa loris*, a synonym.

COMMON WALKING LEAF-FROG
Phyllomedusa burmeisteri

This large (about 3 inches) bright green leaf-frog from central and eastern Brazil currently is unavailable in the hobby, though its bright colors make it quite desirable. This is the major species of a complex of very similar forms distributed over southern South America; these include *Phyllomedusa distincta*

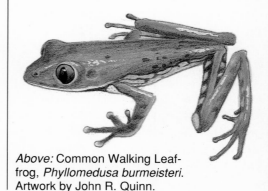

Above: Common Walking Leaf-frog, *Phyllomedusa burmeisteri*. Artwork by John R. Quinn.

from Sao Paulo and *P. tetraploidea*, a form from southern Brazil with an extra set of chromosomes. Also very similar is the Southern Walking Leaf-frog, *P. iheringi*, discussed separately. The belly and side of *P. burmeisteri* are bright yellow, and the hidden surfaces of the legs have dark brown vertical bars. On the side there are short broken brownish lines and bars. The upper lip is white, the eye is dark golden, and there is a long, narrow parotoid gland running from the eye to about half way down the trunk. The tips of the toes are bright yellow.

STARRY LEAF-FROG
Phyllomedusa coelestis

Well over a century ago, noted herpetologist Edward Drinker Cope described a unique leaf-frog from a single specimen from Peru. So far the species, assuming it is valid, has never been rediscovered. The specimen probably was green above, yellow on the side and belly, with dark vertical bars on the side. The hidden surfaces of the hind legs were maroon with yellow spots, while the entire ventral surface was sea-green, without spots. Eye color was not described, but the upper eyelid was said to be yellow-edged. The color sounds much like *Phyllomedusa tomopterna*, but that species has distinct calcars. The vertical dark bars on the sides also sound like species related to *P. hypocondrialis*. Whether the species was based on an aberrant specimen of a known species, represents a badly described known species, or is a "lost" species remains to be determined.

PURPLE-AND-ORANGE LEAF-FROG
Phyllomedusa duellmani

Poorly known, *Phyllomedusa duellmani* is found in the mountains of northern Peru. Adults are about 2 inches long, green on the back and tops of the limbs, and orange with purple dots on the throat and belly. The sides and all hidden limb surfaces are purple with numerous tiny bright orange spots. There is a white stripe running from the jaws along the upper sides. The eye is silvery. This is another of the many beautiful but virtually unknown frogs found in South America in the last 20 years. It seems to lay about 100 eggs in a cluster with the edges of the leaf rolled over the eggs. The eggs are whitish, and there are numerous small water-filled yolkless eggs included in the nest.

AGUA RICA LEAF-FROG
Phyllomedusa ecuatoriana

Described from a unique specimen from the mountains of Ecuador, *Phyllomedusa ecuatoriana* is very similar to *P. duellmani* and *P. perinesos*. It is green above, purplish below, with a white stripe extending back from the eye. The sides and most surfaces of the limbs are purple, with a single large orange blotch on both the anterior and posterior surfaces of the thigh and small orange spots on the upper surfaces of the hands and legs. The eye is silvery. The large orange blotches on the thigh ally it with *P. perinesos*, but the white stripe on the side and presence of at least some orange spots on the feet and hands resemble *P. duellmani*. The species was described from only a single male a bit over 2 inches long. Nothing seems to be reported on its natural history.

ORANGE-LEGGED LEAF-FROG
Phyllomedusa hypocondrialis

   Phyllomedusa hypocondrialis (often misspelled *P. hypochondrialis*) is a pretty leaf-frog that is bright green on the back and tops of the arms and

Occasionally seen in private collections, the Orange-legged Leaf-frog, *Phyllomedusa hypocondrialis*, probably should be kept by only the most experienced hobbyists. It is delicate and difficult to breed, and its food consists of very small insects.

legs, with a distinct yellow-orange stripe on the upper side continued forward as a whitish line over the lips. The throat and belly are white, often with a few black specks on the chest. The sides and hidden surfaces of the legs are bright orange, the sides with irregular broken black bars

or vertically elongated spots, while the upper arms, thighs, and backs of the legs have distinct black bars. The eye is bright silvery yellow. The skin of both the back and belly is weakly granular. Adults are about 1.5 to 2 inches long. The inner two toes are opposable. In many respects this species looks like the related Tiger-striped Leaf-frog (*P. tomopterna*), but that species lacks the pale stripe along the side and is more yellowish than orangish on the legs and sides, as well as having large calcars on the heels.

   The Orange-legged Leaf-frog is one of the most widely distributed frogs, being found over most of South America east of the Andes, from Colombia to Argentina and southern Brazil. It is especially common in prairie-like habitats with sparse trees, bromeliads, and much grass, where it breeds in shallow ponds after the first rains of the rainy season. As usual, males attract females to the pond, they pair up, and then they lay egg clutches on leaves over the water. The edges of the leaf supporting the eggs are drawn together by the female to form a type of case around the mass. An average nest contains about 80 eggs, but it also includes as many as 300 water-filled yolkless eggs that help keep the egg clutch moist during dry periods. The eggs hatch in about eight to nine days.

   Orange-legged Leaf-frogs occasionally are imported and make interesting though delicate terrarium inhabitants. They do not need high humidity to thrive, but do need small insect foods. Never open the nest (i.e., the rolled leaf edges over the eggs) as this will cause the eggs to dry out and the embryos to die. A subspecies, *P. h. azurea,* sometimes is recognized for specimens from Paraquay. The white lip stripe may be reduced, the pattern on the side may include thin brown stripes, and the tadpoles have blue tails heavily spotted with black. *P. centralis*, the Mato Grosso Leaf-frog, is closely related and known only from the Mato Grosso region of Brazil.

SOUTHERN WALKING LEAF-FROG
Phyllomedusa iheringi

This close relative of *Phyllomedusa burmeisteri* occurs in the relatively dry prairies of northern Argentina and adjacent Brazil and Uruguay. Males are about 2.5 inches long, females 3 inches. The inner two toes and fingers are opposable, there is a distinct parotoid gland, and the skin of the back is smooth. The belly is granular and bright yellow with reddish tints, as are the hands and feet. The side has a bright orange band containing violet to maroon reticulations. The hidden surfaces of the legs also are orange with dark short bars or spots. The Southern Walking Leaf-frog is not familiar in captivity.

LEMUR LEAF-FROG
Phyllomedusa lemur

Lemur Leaf-frogs are familiar

subjects of photographs on calendars, cards, and magazine covers, and they are among the few leaf-frogs that have been bred in captivity. Found in moist forests of Costa Rica and Panama, *Phyllomedusa lemur* is closely related to *P. buckleyi* and especially to *P. medinai* of South America. In color it is one of the plainest leaf-frogs, pale green above and creamy white to pale orange below. At night the green becomes brown. Usually there are at least a few small brown specks or freckles on the back during the day, these becoming darker at night. The hidden surfaces of the limbs are pale orange-tan. The eye is striking: large, bulging, and bright silvery white with a broad black ring making them stand out even more. Males usually are about 1.5 inches long, females 2 inches.

Because the region in which they live has rain all year, the frogs are active all year and can be found breeding at any time.

Below: Lemur Leaf-frog, *Phyllomedusa lemur.* Artwork by John R. Quinn.

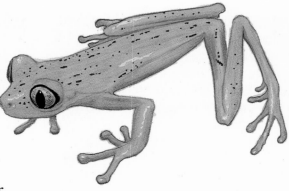

They like plenty of ventilation in the terrarium and prefer rather low temperatures, 75°F (24°C) or less. Considered delicate in the terrarium, they may have been killed by temperatures that were too high. As usual, they hide under leaves of trees during the day and become active at night. Their movements are slow, involving hand-over-hand climbing and few jumps. Males call to attract females to ponds, where mating takes place. The eggs are laid on leaves overhanging the water and the edges of the leaves are not rolled over to make a nest (unlike many other *Phyllomedusa*). Clutches are small, often only 20 or fewer eggs, but females may lay two or more clutches in one mating. There are no small, water-filled yolkless eggs among the pale greenish to bluish yolked eggs. The eggs hatch in one to two weeks, and the tadpoles metamorphose after two to three months. Sexual maturity may be attained in less than a year.

The breeding habits of *P. lemur* and its close relatives are more like those of *Agalychnis* than most *Phyllomedusa*, including not rolling the leaf edges and the absence of yolkless eggs. It even has been suggested that this species and the rest of the *buckleyi* group may represent a distinct genus. Imported specimens occasionally appear in pet shops, but captive-bred young seem to be commercially unavailable.

RANCHO GRANDE LEAF-FROG
Phyllomedusa medinai

This is the Venezuelan version of *Phyllomedusa lemur*. It agrees in most respects with that species, including being green by day and brown by night. There are small brown flecks on the back and usually some larger scattered white spots (absent in *P. lemur*). The hidden surfaces of the limbs are dull orangish brown, as is the belly. The chest and throat are white, and the eye is a pale golden color with a narrow black ring about the edge. Adults are about 2 inches in length, females somewhat longer than males. The snout of this species slopes slightly in front of the nostrils, while in *P. lemur* it is truncate without an obvious slope. The egg clusters contain at least 50 eggs and are deposited under leaves above water; they do not appear to be covered by rolled leaf edges. There is an observation of a small snake, *Liophis reginae*, preying on the eggs. The range as far as known is restricted to cloud forest in Parque Nacional Henri Pittier, more commonly known as Rancho Grande from the biological research station once active there.

JAGUAR LEAF-FROG
Phyllomedusa palliata

The Jaguar Leaf-frog is related to *Phyllomedusa hypocondrialis* and has a somewhat similar color pattern; it is even closer in pattern to *P. rohdei*. Found in the Amazon basin of Ecuador and Peru, it is a small species seldom reaching 2 inches in either sex. The fingers and toes are strongly

Above: Jaguar Leaf-frog, *Phyllomedusa palliata*. Artwork by John R. Quinn.

opposable, and the limbs are slender with small discs. The backs and tops of the limbs are bright green, the belly creamy yellow with small brownish flecks. Along the side from the snout to the groin is a broad whitish band that is heavily marked with large and small brownish spots. In the groin this band becomes orange, as are the hidden surfaces of the limbs. In the groin and on the limbs the orange often is segregated into large spots by a brown reticulation. The eye is bronzy, darker below than above. The eggs number from about 50 to almost 75 and are laid in vegetation above water. Little has been published on its natural history.

ORANGE-SPOTTED LEAF-FROG
Phyllomedusa perinesos

This Ecuadorean leaf-frog is distinguished from *Phyllomedusa duellmani* and other similar species by the color pattern. There is a small calcar at the heel. As

usual for the group, it is green above and purplish below with whitish pustules. The side is dark purple with many small white pustules, while the hidden surfaces of the limbs are purple with large orange spots or blotches. There is no white stripe back from the silvery to faintly greenish eye. The large orange blotches on a purple background are distinctive, but there is quite a bit of variation among the recorded specimens in number and size of blotches. The eggs are laid in masses of about 50 to 75 plus many small water-filled yolkless eggs. The edges of the leaf on which they are laid is rolled over to form a closed nest.

FLECKED LEAF-FROG
Phyllomedusa psilopygion

A close relative of *Phyllomedusa buckleyi* and *P. lemur*, the Flecked Leaf-frog is found in southern Colombia in Pacific slope rainforest. Small calcars are present at the heels. Like related species, it is green above (brown at night), with a whitish belly. There usually are small brownish flecks on the back, these more greenish at night. The sides and hidden surfaces of the limbs are bright orange. A clutch of about 100 grayish tan eggs is recorded, these laid on a rock in a grotto in the rainforest. The species remains virtually unknown.

MERTENS'S LEAF-FROG
Phyllomedusa rohdei

A rather small (males 1.5 inches, females under 2 inches) species from the lowlands of

Below: Mertens's Leaf-frog, *Phyllomedusa rohdei*. Artwork by John R. Quinn.

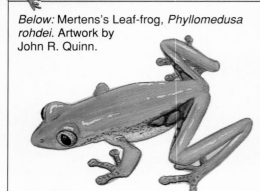

southeastern Brazil, Mertens's Leaf-frog seldom is seen in the hobby. It is closely related to the Orange-legged Leaf-frog but differs in color. The backs and tops of the limbs are green, the belly whitish. There is an indistinct band of fine brown spots on the side in a pale band that starts behind the eye, while the groin and hidden surfaces of the hind legs are bright orange with black bars that often connect to isolate circles of orange. The belly is whitish with fine black specks on the chest. The eggs hatch in about two weeks from a nest with the edges of the leaf folded over the eggs. The tadpoles metamorphose in about six weeks. There is little modern hobby experience with this species because legal exportations from Brazil are prohibited.

WAXY MONKEY FROG
Phyllomedusa sauvagi

The 3-inch-long Waxy Monkey Frog is an inhabitant of the Chaco or dry prairies of northern Argentina and southern Brazil north to adjacent Bolivia and Paraguay. In many ways it resembles the Giant Monkey Frog,

Phyllomedusa bicolor, having the same stout build, large head, and large, toad-like parotoid gland behind the eye. The eye is bronzy with many black flecks. The skin is rough, with many wax glands on the back and pustules on the belly. Overall the color is a dull bluish green above and below, almost unmarked on the back, with a broken white stripe on the upper side and variable white spots and stripes in several rows along the chest and belly. The lower lip is bright white. Juveniles may have orange spots on the hidden surfaces of the groin.

This is one of the leaf-frogs that wipes wax over its skin to prevent desiccation, especially when handled. The wax, as well as other chemicals, is produced in large quantities and is a great adaptation to surviving in the dry habitats frequented by the frog. It usually is found in scraggly trees and shrubs near areas that produce temporary ponds during the infrequent rains. The eggs are laid on leaves over the water as usual, often in very large

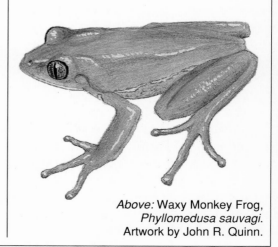

Above: Waxy Monkey Frog, *Phyllomedusa sauvagi*. Artwork by John R. Quinn.

clutches. They are enclosed in a nest made by folding over the edges of the leaf and are plugged with small water-eggs. In captivity adults have eaten small beetles and crickets, but they are difficult to maintain. If you should run across a specimen in the pet shop, try providing a low humidity and relatively high temperatures—it might work.

BROWN-BELLIED LEAF-FROG
Phyllomedusa tarsius

This large (males 3.5 inches, females 4 inches or more), rough-skinned leaf-frog is found from Colombia to Peru in the Amazon basin. The closely related (almost identical) *Phyllomedusa venusta* and *P. trinitatis* occur to the northwest and northeast of this species and are best separated by locality. There are long parotoid glands extending back from the eye almost to the groin, while large adults have white tubercles at the edges of the limbs. The back, sides of the head, and tops of the limbs are bright green, while the throat and chest are brown with a median white spot on the chest; the belly is dull

Above: Brown-bellied Leaf-frog, *Phyllomedusa tarsius.* Artwork by John R. Quinn.

orange. The side is marked with numerous whitish to orangish spots and blotches that may fuse into an indistinct band, while the hidden surfaces of the limbs are pale tan to orangish with scattered whitish to greenish spots. The eye is bright gold with black flecks. This is a very variable species both with age and from locality to locality, and doubtless it hides several similar species. There are quite a few synonyms. This is a species of tall trees, where it often calls from many feet above the ground. It lays large clutches of eggs on leaves folded over into a nest. Hatching takes seven or eight days.

TIGER-STRIPED LEAF-FROG
Phyllomedusa tomopterna

This lovely leaf-frog has been kept and bred quite often in Europe but appears to be virtually unavailable on the American market. It is one of the most strikingly colored species, being bright green above with a bright yellow belly and white throat. The sides, hands, feet, and hidden surfaces of the limbs are bright yellow with numerous vertical black bars of varied thicknesses, sometimes broken and partially connected. The eye is silvery gray, sometimes finely flecked with black. The whole body often appears waxy. Adult males are about 2 inches long, females 2.5 inches.

Widely distributed over much of northern and central South America, it is a species of the rainforest, hiding by day under

PHOTO BY PAUL FREED.

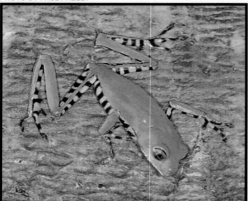

Popular in Europe but virtually never seen in the United States, the Tiger-striped Leaf-frog, *Phyllomedusa tomopterna*, is thought by the author to be a "good buy" and worthy of further investigation by hobbyists. Males are about 2 inches long, females just a bit larger, and specimens apparently respond well to captive living.

leaves and in shrubs and coming out at night. Most success has come from keeping this species rather cool (75°F, 24°C) most of the year and letting the humidity run between 50 and 70%. It needs good ventilation, not stagnant, saturated tropical air. Females lay clutches of about 100 eggs on leaves over the water and then roll the edges of the leaf over the clutch to make a closed nest. Hatching takes about nine or ten days, and the tadpoles are ready to metamorphose about two months later. They leave the water with a well-developed tail and hide until the tail is absorbed, when they begin feeding. Adult coloration may take a month to develop, and sexual maturity arrives in about a year.

This is one of the few leaf-frogs

with a well-developed calcar, a pointed flap of skin on the heel. (Others include *Agalychnis calcarifer*, *A. craspedopus*, *Phyllomedusa buckleyi*, *P. psilopygion*, and some *Phrynomedusa* and *Phasmahyla* species.) This character in combination with the distinctive coloration makes it hard to misidentify. Importations are found occasionally in pet shops and might be a good buy.

TRINIDAD LEAF-FROG
Phyllomedusa trinitatis

This leaf-frog from the coast of Venezuela and the adjacent island of Trinidad has indistinct parotoid glands but otherwise looks much like *Phyllomedusa tarsius*. The chin and chest are brown, the back green. Like other relatives of *P. tarsius*, it may be best identified by locality. Its eggs are laid on leaves hanging over the water as usual, but often several leaves are pulled together to cover the nest instead of just one as in the Orange-legged Leaf-frog. There are many small water-filled yolkless eggs at the top and bottom of the egg mass. The eggs often are left partially exposed and seem more resistant to dehydration than in some other species that build leaf nests or cones.

WHITE-LINE LEAF-FROG
Phyllomedusa vaillanti

A distinctive and widely distributed species, the White-line Leaf-frog is found over much of South America from the Guianas and Colombia south to northern

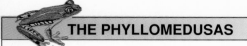
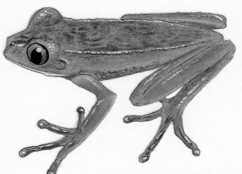

Above: White-line Leaf-frog,
Phyllomedusa vaillanti.
Artwork by John R. Quinn.

Peru and Bolivia. Adult males are about 2 inches long, females often over 3 inches. The back and sides of the head, as well as the upper side, are bright green, the skin rough. The parotoid gland extends back from the eye as a fine ridge marked with numerous white pustules that make up the thin white line for which the species is named. The lower side is reddish brown with a row of whitish to orangish spots separating it from the green upper side. The reddish brown coloration extends to cover the hidden surfaces of the limbs, which also have scattered small whitish to orangish spots. There is a distinctive pattern on the underside, but it varies a bit with age and has caused juveniles to be described as distinct species. In young the belly is dull orange with an indistinct network of grayish lines. In adults the ventral pattern is more complicated, being largely brownish with a large green spot at the center of the chest and a pair of creamy spots on the throat (somewhat resembling the pattern in *Phyllomedusa tarsius* and allies).

Unfortunately, little has been published on its natural history, but it lays clutches of eggs on leaves above water as usual for the genus. Surprisingly, considering its broad range, it does not appear regularly in the terrarium hobby.

LOVELY LEAF-FROG
Phyllomedusa venusta

One of the most poorly known leaf-frogs, *Phyllomedusa venusta* was described from western Panama and remains rare. It is big, with males often 3.5 inches long and females 4 inches, has rough skin, and has a long parotoid gland that extends as a line almost to the back leg. Green on the back and the tops of the limbs, it is brown on the throat and chest and dull orange on the belly; there is a large white spot in the center of the chest. The hidden surfaces of the legs are pinkish orange with some greenish brown and orange flecks. The sides are green with tiny blue specks. The bright golden eye has many black specks. There are white pustules on the edges of the hind legs. This species is closely related to the South American *P. tarsius*, differing mostly in minor details of coloration.

The type specimens were taken in a swampy area during light showers and did not show any evidence of mating. Males lack vocal slits and thus may lack an audible call note.

The author will provide bibliographic assistance to interested hobbyists who wish to contact him through T.F.H. Publications.

OTHER T.F.H. BOOKS BY THE AUTHOR

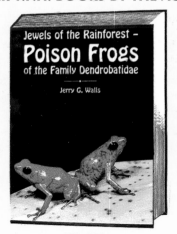

TS-223

LR-106

TS-144

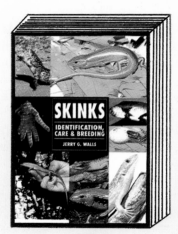

RE-111

RE-110

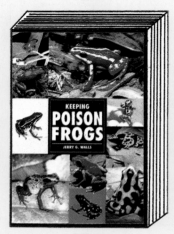

RE-108

These and hundreds of other colorful and informative pet-keeping books are available from T.F.H. Publications. Check your local pet shop for more titles.